# 003

Published
April 2016

Title
Extra Ordinary

Author
Allford Hall Monaghan Morris
/ Simon Allford

ISBN
978-0-9934378-0-9

Design
Graphic Thought Facility

Printer
Pureprint

Specification
116.25 x 155mm, 138pp
Typeset in Unica77
Munken Lynx smooth 240gsm
Munken Lynx Smooth 100gsm
Chorus Lux Gloss 130gsm
Takeo Tant Select Ts.3 s-3

FifthMan

# Extra Ordinary

## Some thoughts on architecture and the theatre of everyday life

Mies van der Rohe said: 'I don't want to be interesting. I just want to be good.'

Or, as our tutor David Dunster once said to me of a student project, 'it's boring - which is good; but unfortunately it's not boring enough!' So boring can be good. Or put another way, ordinary buildings are good. They are fundamental to successful urbanity.

We should have a positive attitude to the ordinary – and the particular qualities of very good ordinary buildings that identify them as extra ordinary.

Donald Judd's home at 101 Spring Street in New York, for example, was originally a commercial cast-iron building. The straightforward but structured spaces inside and the confident rhythmic detailing of the facade have, as identified by Judd's occupation, proven themselves to be extra ordinary.

Vast tracts of London are similarly distinguished by the elegant banality and repetition that makes them extra ordinary. London's squares and terraces (and, further north, ladders and warrens) of Georgian and Victorian housing were all designed by developers following a pattern book, with architects retreating to the bastions of cultural production.

The raw industrial space of Donald Judd's nineteenth-century garment factory in New York became a permanent installation of his work. It is now the only cast-iron building in SoHo that retains a single use – as a public gallery.

Similarly, the modern vernacular as pioneered by Mies is, in his hands, extra ordinary. The ultimate refinement of this is the Seagram Building, endlessly copied but never bettered. It is a contextual response, and is the culmination of his journey from classicism to sheer glass fantasies, on through opulent veneers and brick expressionism to his particular take on the ancient idea of frame and infill.

Nothing of course is as simple as that. The concrete encasement conceals a steel frame which is then expressed in bronze. It is rigidly logical in its expression of the technology of construction, but it also demonstrates the importance of the idea. Mies acknowledged this. After a two-hour lecture justifying the technical logic, he concluded by noting that, 'of course we did it that way as we best liked the way it looked'.

Completed in 1958, the 39-storey Seagram Building was intended as a headquarters for the Seagram distillery company. They only needed the first six floors of the tower, the remainder being designed speculatively for other commercial tenants who in effect subsidised the building.

2

Mies' School of Architecture at the Illinois Institute of Technology (IIT) is an equally well-proportioned, elegant space which allows activity to happen. It doesn't have any sort of agenda, political or otherwise, but that doesn't matter. Mies' interest was in 'universal space' – space designed to be appropriated by programmes that were yet to be defined or discovered.

Architecture cannot control the life of the building in use, and nor should the architect seek to do so.

Now known as SR Crown Hall, Mies van der Rohe's 1956 School of Architecture was intended to be a 'home for ideas and adventures'.

Extra ordinary buildings withstand the winds of political and ideological change. The Casa del Fascio in Como, renamed following a post-war switch of ideologies as the Casa del Popolo, continues to be referenced and revered regardless of the politics of its commission or use.

This suggests that the politics of the building are less important than the building itself. A building is simply either bad, good or, better still, extra ordinary.

Giuseppe Terragni's 1936 Casa del Fascio in Como, Italy, was built as the headquarters of the local Fascist Party. Having formed a rationalist stage set for fascist rallies during the second world war, it was renamed the Casa del Popolo (House of the People) and restored to civic service as a police station, tax office and museum.

Extra ordinary buildings in the city are memorable because they not only define important urban space externally, but also internally. They survive and endure because they are extra ordinary without and within. They have intrinsic personality. They display a tension between the generic and specific, and – like the Casa del Fascio – continue to be relevant because they are neither restrictive of use nor defined by it. Instead, they allow their owners and occupants to perform as they wish, yet their specific qualities also inform and challenge the imagination of the occupants.

The Bradbury Building is the oldest commercial building in the centre of Los Angeles, USA. Designed by Sumner Hunt, it was commissioned by mining millionaire Lewis Bradbury, who wanted a grand office building to anchor his real estate empire, and was completed by George Wyman in 1893. Behind the modest sandstone exterior is an exuberant Victorian central court, galleried with wrought-iron staircases and railings. The building has been used as a location for more than twenty films, including Ridley Scott's 1982 dystopian *Blade Runner* and (as a movie studio) in the 2011 silent film *The Artist*.

These buildings tend not to have a signature. The identity of the author, the architect, the owner – or any mixture of these – is not always evident.

In 1953, sculptor Phyllis Lambert (shown right in the picture) was so fervently unimpressed with her father's plans for a New York sky-scraper on Park Avenue that she joined his team as director of planning. With Philip Johnson (left), she drew up a list of candidates for the design of the building, finally selecting Mies van der Rohe (centre) as architect. She defended his vision throughout its construction. 'Mies forces you in,' she wrote at the time. 'You might think this austere strength, this ugly beauty, is terribly severe. It is, and yet all the more beauty in it.'

Since the virtual world became ubiquitous, there's been much debate on the effect of this on our real, physical world. About how manoeuvring in a parallel, digital realm will de-structure and destabilise the city, and how the internet will free us from urban life. Whereas, in actuality, people have continued to flood to cities in ever greater numbers.

The headquarters building for London Underground at 55 Broadway was, at 53.3 metres, the tallest in London when completed in 1929. The design of the Grade I-listed building by Charles Holden was influenced by similar office structures in New York and Chicago, in its use of a reinforced concrete system but also in the way it embodied the corporate values of a large organisation.

Cities continue to be social condensers, places of chance encounter. And as buildings come and go over time, it is the places in between, the permanent streets, that are most important. Buildings are significant only in that they help define the character of the streets and suggest the culture of their era.

The Mall is the only formal feature in the whole of Central Park, WNew York, and was once described as an 'open air hall of reception'. During the nineteenth century it was a favourite promenade for wealthy Manhattanites, who would be dropped from their carriages at one end and picked up at the other once their walk was complete.

The city is the subject of endless analysis and theoretical thinking. It's defined through numerous lenses: as a network, as a cluster of cultures, activities, people, businesses, and as a reflection of the governance of visible and invisible systems.

Guy Debord's 1957 map *The Naked City* reconfigures the rational city grid as a psychogeography, with discrete neighbourhood hubs networked by desire lines and 'drift' between these hubs at a single moment in time.

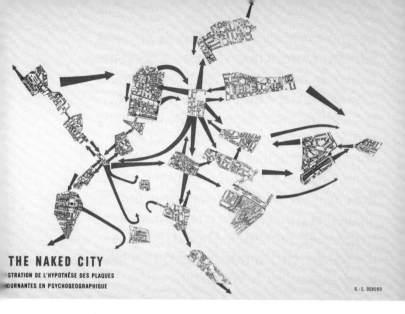

**THE NAKED CITY**
ISTRATION DE L'HYPOTHÉSE DES PLAQUES
OURNANTES EN PSYCHOGEOGRAPHIQUE

G. - E. DEBORD

9

But the city is also defined by its physical infrastructure. It is structured around the spaces in between, so why do architects – who like to think they are creating cities – not seek an involvement at the beginning rather than at the end of long and ambitious infrastructure projects? The design of the physical infrastructure that services the city is an ever more important and challenging project. As cities evolve into megacities, architects should reassert the relevance of strategic design thinking to infrastructure, from the off.

Louis Kahn's 1953 traffic study for his home city of Philadelphia, USA, became an incredibly detailed investigation of movement throughout the city, but was founded on clear strategic metaphors. He likened the expressways to rivers framing a medieval European city, with parking towers as bastions in between.

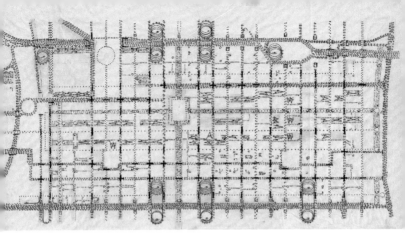

Of course there is also a nineteenth-century idea of the city mimicking nature, capturing an invented and parallel rural arcadia. The spaces in between become artificial fragments of the pastoral, serving to create a different version of the relationship between the inhabitants of the city and the world of nature beyond it.

Agnes Denes's work *Wheatfield – A Confrontation* was created in 1982 as two acres of wheat on a landfill site in lower Manhattan (now Battery Park City and the World Financial Center). Planted on a site worth $4.5 billion to developers, the wheatfield worked to challenge issues around waste, hunger and ecology, as well as creating a powerful evocation of the countryside in the heart of one of the world's largest cities.

Cities are also places of collective memory, so associations and connections back to those memories of place and use are vital. The specific qualities of extra ordinary buildings offer a physical link to the past while continuing to define, or at least inform, activities into the future. This is why historical context and sense of place must still inform our approach when we are designing. Even when building anew we are building on history.

On 29 December 1940, after a day of heavy bombing, photographer Herbert Mason took three images of St Paul's Cathedral from the roof of the Daily Mail building on Fleet Street. Cropped, and with alterations to place more emphasis on the cathedral dome, the image was finally published by the Daily Mail two days later as a symbol of defiance, with the headline 'War's Greatest Picture: St Paul's stands unharmed in the midst of the burning city'. Three weeks later, the Berliner Illustrierte Zeitung used the same image on its front cover to show the destruction of the city, with the title 'Die City von London brennt' ('The City of London burns').

Challenging this idea of a universal programme of use is the notion that place helps define what we do and how we do it. In turn, activity (work or domestic) also helps define place. Shoreditch in east London, for example, was a centre for furniture-making in the early twentieth century: it was cheaper to make furniture there than elsewhere (even Liverpool!). And furniture-making has continued to define Shoreditch into the early twenty-first century. The programme of use dictated the size and scale of buildings, and these continue to define the area's character. So there emerges a contrary idea that use also defines cities and how we think about them. And if cities define how we think about architecture, then use becomes important to us.

In 1801, there was just one furniture firm on Curtain Road in Shoreditch, but with the opening of the East and West India docks, connected by canals to east London, hundreds of small workshops opened up in the neighbourhood. By the end of the nineteenth century, furniture-making employed tens of thousands of people in the area.

The way in which we draw patterns of use in cities can actually define how we subsequently read them and therefore what they become. We usually represent and analyse the city in plan, yet this cannot possibly show the full picture of activity in a sectional city. The postwar zoning proposal for Shoreditch is a flavourless abstract compared to the richly varied map of prewar use. But even this earlier record is inaccurate because it cannot show the sectional mix of activity, the homes and warehouses above work-shops and studios.

The County of London plan was commissioned in 1941 and, despite there being no end to the war in sight, it was clear that the bombing of London during those early years would offer an opportunity to rethink the city once peace returned. Ernő Goldfinger and EJ Carter's condensed version of the plan was published by Penguin in 1945 as an explanation to the earlier document. It includes a glossary of useful terms including a definition of the architect who 'traditionally makes his buildings not merely efficient but also beautiful'.

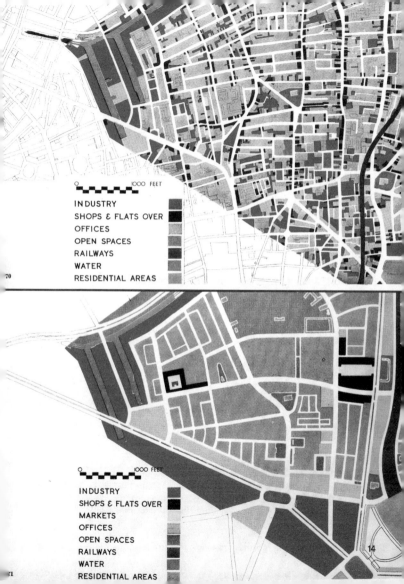

O _____ 1000 FEET

INDUSTRY
SHOPS & FLATS OVER
OFFICES
OPEN SPACES
RAILWAYS
WATER
RESIDENTIAL AREAS

70

O _____ 1000 FEET

INDUSTRY
SHOPS & FLATS OVER
MARKETS
OFFICES
OPEN SPACES
RAILWAYS
WATER
RESIDENTIAL AREAS

14

71

Cities are also defined by a framework of governance. The regulations within which we all work are a lowest common denominator to which we all refer. You can measure a building in terms of floor area, and you can even measure it in terms of cost, or volume, or light, but the regulations do not incorporate any measures for the quality of experience or the pleasure it might offer.

The danger of all regulations – in fact, any overriding patterns of logic – is that they gum up the conversation about what architecture is. And, of course, architectural design is defined as much by the irrational as the rational.

James Gillray's 1787 etching *A March to the Bank* shows the daily march of the Bank of England's own military guard, two abreast, up the Strand and along Fleet Street to their stations. The public were so incensed by their jostling, orders were eventually given for the guard to move only in single file. The illustration seems to sit well with journalist HL Mencken's statement, a hundred years later in his *In Defense of Women*, that, 'the whole aim of practical politics is to keep the populace alarmed'.

Good buildings, extra ordinary buildings, therefore flex. They flex over time, mimicking the city and the all-important spaces in between. These buildings have some permanent characteristics but they also offer latitude for great change, allowing for uses that we can't yet predict – and which we shouldn't really wish to prescribe. Which only highlights the absurdity of the regulation of specific 'use-less class orders' and demonstrates the need for an alternative 'Universal Use Class Order'.

The Town and Country Planning Order 1987 puts building uses into a series of categories known as use classes. A new 'Universal Use Class' would allow buildings to flex in response to activity rather than setting out a specific menu of functions.

# *Town and Country Planning Act 2012*

## Universal Use Class Orders
### *with supplementary Building Licences*

We now live in a world where people like to talk about 'creatives'. What's interesting is that the same factories where the workers used to crowd through the gates at the beginning and end of the working day, pursuing supposedly monotonous de-skilled activity, are now being adapted for a completely different use by a new generation of creatives. Factories are newly relevant and the distinction between creative and 'non-creative' business in the twenty-first century is ever more irrelevant.

In 1841, almost 36 per cent of the England and Wales workforce was employed in manufacturing, usually in large factories. By 2011, just 9 per cent worked in manufacturing, with 81 per cent of the workforce employed in the services industries. Of these, 2.3 million people were employed in the creative economy, increasing to 2.6 million in 2013.

17

The Tea Building in Shoreditch is a good example of a factory building being continuously redefined and reinvented. As architects we actually did nothing more than enable new suites of activities to emerge. This 'non-plan' idea is perhaps better than the related, and potentially creepy, emerging idea that we 'curate' projects and thus we 'curate' communities.

The Tea Building was built in the 1930s as a bacon curing factory for Lipton, and then – with the Biscuit Building next door – adapted for tea packing. During the 1970s it was taken over by Securicor as a storage warehouse. Since then it has been used as a nightclub and gallery space, and now houses almost fifty work units and offices of differing sizes, most of them occupied by creative and media companies. At ground floor there are restaurants, and upstairs is Shoreditch House, a private members' club.

The current fascination with buildings as objects (where often the only real programme is to be an object) …

Architect and mathematician Lionel March has used applied maths to examine the quantitative relationships between building forms, heights, areas of sites – and the spaces in between them.

... highlights one of the great problems of post-functionalist twenty-first century architecture.

What we actually need to acknowledge is that the public space is key; that buildings are in fact just the volumes in between the spaces (and not the other way round!). Too often cities are planned diagrammatically, according to regulations and rules, and without vision or under-standing of a city's inherent character.

Ebenezer Howard's Garden City was structured as a series of vast concentric rings, segmented by wide boulevards and circled by an industrial zone of factories and works. Civic buildings and a park were placed at the centre of the city. The strictly geometric plan did not offer a suggestion as to the form or massing of the buildings, or the spaces in between them.

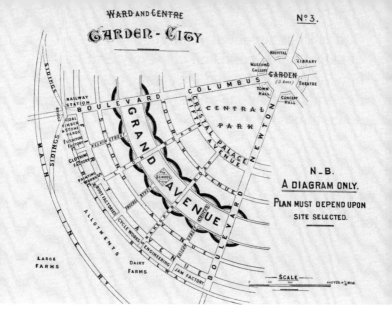

WARD AND CENTRE

# GARDEN - CITY

HOSPITAL

LIBRARY

MUSEUM & GALLERY

GARDEN (5 Acres)

THEATRE

TOWN HALL

CONCERT HALL

BOULEVARD COLUMBUS

CRYSTAL PALACE

FIFTH AVENUE

CENTRAL PARK

NEWTON

RAILWAY STATION

COAL TIMBER & STONE YARDS

FURNITURE FACTORY

CLOTHING FACTORY

PRINTING WORKS

BOOT FACTORIES

CYCLE WORKS & ENGINEERING

JAM FACTORY

KELVIN STREET

FIFTH AVENUE

BOULEVARD

GRAND AVENUE

SCHOOL

SIDINGS

MAIN LINE RY

ALLOTMENTS

RAILWAY

LARGE FARMS

DAIRY FARMS

N - B.
A DIAGRAM ONLY.
PLAN MUST DEPEND UPON
SITE SELECTED.

SCALE

440 YDS. = ½ MILE.

Cedric Price repeatedly turned to the question of the condition of the city, and how it might be defined. He appreciated its complexity and the need to leave some things to chance.

Cedric Price drew the city as an egg: boiled in ancient times and organised around a central 'yolk'; fried more haphazardly during the seventeenth to nineteenth centuries, and finally scrambled into the modern metropolis.

# THE CITY AS AN EGG

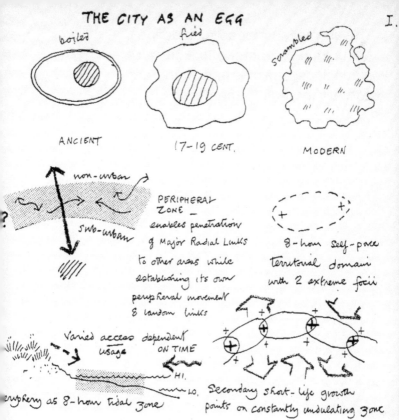

boiled
ANCIENT

fried
17–19 CENT.

scrambled
MODERN

non-urban
sub-urban
?

PERIPHERAL ZONE – enables penetration of Major Radial Links to other areas while establishing its own peripheral movement & random links

8-hour self-pace territorial domain with 2 extreme focii

Varied access dependent on usage ON TIME

periphery as 8-hour tidal zone

HI.
LO.

Secondary short-life growth points on constantly undulating zone

# EDRIC PRICE PROPOSITIONS

The un-measurables which define the unique character of the city as a place of use, misuse and abuse, are actually incredibly important.

*London Night and Day,* illustrated by Osbert Lancaster, offers a far more engaging description of the city than many maps, plans and sections of the period. As 'a guide to where the other books don't take you', it leads the reader around the lesser-known sights of 1950s London and is organised by the hour to reveal the changing life of the city over time.

# LONDON
## NIGHT AND DAY

### illustrated by Osbert Lancaster
#### edited by Sam Lambert

5/- net   *A GUIDE TO WHERE THE OTHER*   5/- net
*BOOKS DON'T TAKE YOU*

People have opted to congregate in cities for over two millennia. They're drawn by the promise of wealth, entertainment and possibility. This challenges the idea of designing for specific use. But how do you build in the irrational, the chance encounter?

The London Group is a progressive society of artists, founded in 1913 as an alternative to the Royal Academy for the exhibition of new work. Famously, the group makes no judgemental decisions on the output of its members. Sculptor John Skeaping, the first husband of Barbara Hepworth was drawn to London – and the group    during the 1920s, and is shown here feeding an elephant in London Zoo while his drawing scholars look on.

And what happens when a city is unsuccessful? There's a long and continuing history of urban blight, most clearly exemplified in recent times by Detroit. When the car industry failed the city did too. Did Detroit fail because there was something inherently wrong with its design? Or did it fail simply because of the mobility of Americans who (certainly by comparison with the English) will, when economic circumstances dictate, move on to another city or state.

Detroit's prosperity during the first half of the twentieth century was based on the motor trade, with large manufacturing plants for Ford, Chrysler, Packard and many others all located in the city. With the gradual decline of the US auto industry, the city's economy and population have also declined. Thousands of buildings across Detroit have been abandoned, with the population now the same size – 700,000 – as it was in 1910 before large-scale motor manufacture began, a fall of 60 per cent since the population peaked at 1.86 million in 1950. One in three Detroit residents lives in poverty.

So we congregate in cities to socialise, civilise, engage. We come together to be creative and, through that creativity, generate fame or fortune and ideally both. And, in a way, that spirit of creativity is what we ought to be looking to cultivate in any building we design. That's why the internet hasn't managed to transform our understanding of, or our need to congregate in, cities – we are social beasts and we need to interact in a physical environment.

During August each year, a field in Ballintaggart, County Kerry, becomes a temporary city for the Dingle Races. The impromptu meet attracts huge numbers of horses, riders and spectators from across Ireland and beyond.

A few years ago we were told that cities would decline and that we should be both able and willing to live in barns in rural arcadia (Wales, that is!) and communicate by email. Now the idea of a place called London is that it is an international city where you must spend time.

We commute in order to communicate. You might live somewhere else, but there will always be times when you have to come to this place, and that's why organisations of every size – even the digital giants – still have desks, and still try to get people together in buildings. We have chosen not to live in the arcadia that was to be enabled by the internet because we need to engage face-to-face (and the internet can be lonely and mind-numbing).

Global internet traffic has grown exponentially in recent years. In May 2015, Cisco predicted that annual global IP traffic would exceed a zetta-byte (or one sextillion ($10^{21}$) bytes) in 2016 and two zettabytes in 2019. It has increased more than fivefold in the past five years.

The environments enjoyed by the new creative industries of twenty-first century London would be quite familiar to Hogarth and Pepys. Nourished by cycle cafes and informal encounters, beanbags and table football, the caffeine culture of Shoreditch is only the latest reincarnation of the old gin palaces and older coffee houses. It's work disguised as socialising and it's an old model, endlessly redescribed by each generation in its arrogance and ignorance of the fact that, every thirty years, we once again re-interpret the past.

William Hogarth's *A Midnight Modern Conversation* is a satirical representation of the drinking clubs that became popular in early eighteenth-century London. With increasing numbers of enfranchised professional gentlemen in the city, clubs became popular as a place for drinking and gambling, although many were also connected with the sporting, cultural or business interests of their members.

Joseph Gandy's painting, which imagines the virtual city of Sir John Soane, suggests the significance of a collection of buildings, placed in array. But it's not the buildings that are important; it's the relationship between them and the spaces in between where the real business of the city takes place.

For more than thirty-five years, Joseph Gandy translated John Soane's architectural ideas into perspective watercolours, either to help sell design ideas to clients or to show his completed work. The largest of these watercolours, *Selection of public and private buildings' parts according to Sir John Soane's projects RA. FSA., for the metropolis and other places of the United Kingdom between 1780 and 1815*, was painted towards the end of Soane's career, and imagined London as an entire city composed of his buildings – as well as some of Gandy's own painted representations.

And this takes us back to the idea that public space is more important than the objects around it. There's an interesting tension in London, focused around the notion that we are witnessing the privatisation of this public space – think of places like Broadgate and Kings Cross. Whereas, in fact, large expanses of public space have often been initiated as private space. Both Broadgate and Kings Cross actually represent the opening up of previously privatised spaces. We should beware the (often false) orthodoxies of the day.

The ancient city of Petra, in Jordan, has very few freestanding buildings. Its main surviving civic structures – treasury, amphitheatre and monastery – are actually carved out of the rock, while most of its public spaces – including the narrow, winding siq which leads into the city from the east – are defined by the topography of the natural landscape.

Giambattista Nolli's map of Rome is interesting because it reveals the churches as important places of public congregation. What would a twenty-first century Nolli map of London expose? What would the public rooms be in a city where the importance of the church has declined? Would they be the pubs or clubs or schools or places of work? They certainly wouldn't be the silent internet cafes. Perhaps only the streets and reinvented shops would be public rooms.

Nolli drew his 1748 map of Rome as a figure-ground plan, with open squares and streets shown as white areas between the shaded buildings. In a revolutionary piece of mapping, he also left the interiors of other civic structures, such as churches and colonnades, unshaded to reveal these as 'public rooms' too. By representing them as positive space, Nolli suggested that it is those in-between spaces, rather than the built objects, that we experience most strongly.

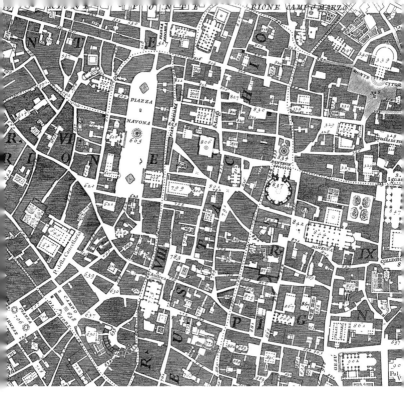

In 1986, Jonathan Hall, Paul Monaghan, Peter Morris and I completed our final-year thesis – *The Fifth Man* – at the Bartlett in London and our research interrogated ideas of the city. We looked at the grid, and the scale of the plot, and how these plots relate to each other as part of a wider fabric. We discussed the efficiency of the planned, gridded city, and how this should be challenged to make creative cities. We accepted the programme as secondary: use was of less import than idea of place.

Generic city plan from *The Fifth Man*, 1986.

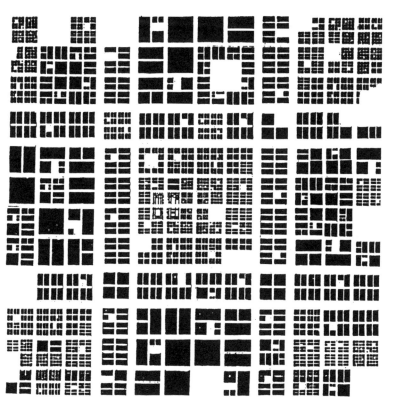

The Fifth Man was about making a play on Mondrian and the city, the life and jazz of his *Broadgate Boogie Woogie* ...

For the four of us (who founded AHMM three years later) Manhattan only works where the grid breaks down, at the edges where it hits the river and where it is intersected by Broadway.

Broadway traces an old Native American trail across Manhattan Island, a route subsequently adopted by Dutch settlers from Nieuw Amsterdam.

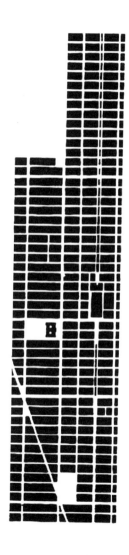

Whereas London works because it is actually a planned city (well actually lots of little plans), scrambled like an egg so different estates clash in different ways. Its present success – and I don't know whether that will endure – is because of these sites of collision, which just don't exist at the same intensity in New York City.

Comparative plans of London and New York City from *The Fifth Man*, 1986.

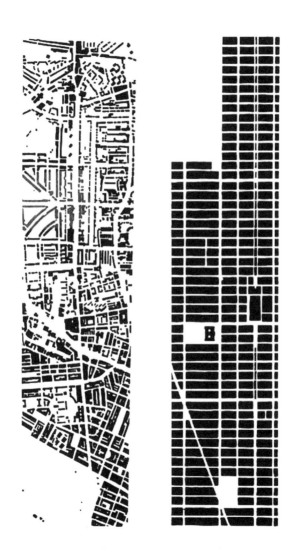

Going back to the idea of infrastructure in the city, what will transform London more than architecture is infrastructure. Projects like the Jubilee Line extension which has connected Westminster to places like Bermondsey, Crossrail which will connect east to west at speed, and the Overground linking Hackney to Crystal Palace. Nothing architecture does can initiate transformations on this kind of scale.

Crossrail will increase rail capacity in London by 10 per cent, carrying around 200 million passengers each year. The east-west rail route is not a new idea. As early as the nineteenth century, industrialists proposed building a cross-capital railway to connect Kings Cross and Paddington with the docks in the east.

All this raises a problem for us as architects. If our briefs are irrelevant, and buildings are more important for what they define without than how they work within, why are we still making buildings?

Presumably because not only do we want to, but others want us to. And if we want to make useful buildings (full of uses), we need to think about what the real drivers of the brief are. I am less and less interested in the secret architectural brief that some wish to pursue, and more interested in the relevance of longevity and the idea that building stock could be designed smarter to last better and longer. Reassuringly for architects and architecture, buildings that are going to last have to be flexible and adaptable, but also memorable. Otherwise why keep them? No-one is engaged by an empty husk.

So what defines the infinitely flexible and adaptable, and the necessarily memorable? For me it starts with the idea of place and address – the way the building works as a place within the wider address of the city.

Filippo Brunelleschi's terracotta-tiled dome dominates the Florence skyline and has become a point of origin around which the Italian city is oriented.

And then it's about the architecture, and how it makes a presence at that address. It's about developing an idea of surface and skin that goes beyond the 'nailing on of elevations', an idea that invites – and gets – an emotional reaction from passers-by.

It's also about promenade. An endlessly flexible building requires an interior with memorable characteristics of circulation and movement. The architect has to create a journey between the street and the stack of ever-changing uses inside.

Certain spaces inside have to become places. There have to be memorable and important locations within the building, just as there are memorable squares, streets and corners in the city. These spaces will also change over time, but at a slower rate, and need to be defined, as much by their character as their light and volume.

38

Buildings should become more open, welcoming and social too. And freely accessible. Perhaps in this sense alone they mirror the internet – but only in as much as the internet mirrors the public realm of the city.

Our attitude to the importance of use in the design of buildings must change, and now!

Places of work (offices), of play (leisure) and of learning (schools) are rapidly becoming indistinguishable. The buildings we are designing must work harder and longer, and so will inevitably be used in very different ways over time. It is essential that we design to accommodate a multitude of uses concurrently and coincidentally across the course of a day, a week, a season, a year.

40

Buildings should embody this urban idea and mirror the success of the city, accommodating communities of varying uses and acting as a backdrop to the life of its inhabitants.

The essential urban building of the near future is flexible, memorable, and allows a mix of programmes to flourish. And it offers Universal Use!

It is a city within a city, defined by the quality of its volume, light, serviceability and attitude to technology. This building of the future is here now and has been for a while, since the Renaissance in fact. The office of the future is the Uffizi in Florence.

Of course, the Uffizi was not just an office for the Medicis. It was also their palace. A civic symbol and a working building. It was a place of work and business; a court but also a home with accommodation for noble families and their retinues. It's now an art gallery, but it always was. Importantly it also encloses a new place in the city.

This building's longevity demonstrates the need to maintain a view on the tension between the generic and the specific. The current Uffizi holds traces of all the previous incarnations of the building's use, and is richer for it.

Giorgio Vasari began the Uffizi in Florence in 1560. The building (as shown on this, and previous, pages) is composed as a model street, the inner facades tiered with identical, repeating window surrounds and strong horizontal courses, which create a trick of perspective and elongate the run of the central courtyard between them and the River Arno beyond. This isn't the building's only connection with the wider city. The Vasari Corridor, a private, elevated and covered walkway connecting the Palazzo Vecchio with the Palazzo Pitti, runs right through the Uffizi, on along the Arno and across the Ponte Vecchio.

Extra ordinary buildings of Universal Use resolve the tension between the generic and specific, and ideas of space and place.

Extra ordinary architecture is informed by a consideration of time. For us, this begins with the idea of the *theatre*, a setting for everyday life, and an object in the city that should last for a hundred years and beyond. It is subject to forces of change which are acknowledged by *stage sets*, buildings within a building that accommodate specific needs and that may last for up to twenty years. These resolve the tension between the generics of the city and the specific needs of the user. The changing needs of everyday life are then addressed by *props*, architectural furniture that allows universal space to be reconfigured. It is this tripartite arrangement that allows a building to be both endlessly reconfigurable and architecturally memorable.

*Theatre, stage set and props*: the architectural brief for extra ordinary buildings required by the Universal Use Class Order – as imagined by AHMM, 2014.

Cedric Price said: 'We should not only be interested in the design of bridges; we should be concerned with how best to get to the other side.'

Or, put another way, what 'brief' should we utilise when we design buildings? What is the real programme? How should we try to ameliorate the immediate needs of the client with the necessarily longer term vision of the building in the city?

The Tees Transporter Bridge was opened in 1911 and is the longest working example of its type in the world. It was designed to replace the crowded ferries which shuttled workers between Middlesbrough and the factories and docks on the northern shore of the Tees. Passengers and vehicles travel in a gondola suspended from a frame, and pulled by cables along the main boom of the structure. The Grade II*-listed bridge has a span of 174 metres.

*Merzbau, Palimpsest, Collage,* the exhibition that AHMM created for the 2014 Venice Biennale, explored this idea of the 'long history of architecture'.

Timothy Soar's photographs, along with a table of ephemera, revealed traces of the past life of the city in twelve recent AHMM projects. In mapping the history that continues to inform these projects, be they reutilisation, reinvention or new build, what was clear was that ideas of use were a lot less important than ideas of how the architect of the city accommodates the ever changing theatre of everyday life.

The Angel Building's central atrium is the imprint of the courtyard within its 1980s structural frame, which itself related to the yard within a nineteenth-century coaching inn which previously stood on the site.

46

The Barbican project was about imagining the continual reinhabitation of a mega-structure, a megastructure that has gone out of fashion ... and come back in again.

art/theatre/music
dance/film/education
conferences/library
restaurants/bars

47

Barking Central is a newer piece of city, and here a suite of buildings has been built around a public room – a landscaped park.

Television Centre in west London will be a new city quarter that retains memories of the heyday of the BBC as well as re-housing remaining fragments of the vast array of studios.

49

The Battleship Building – formerly a maintenance depot for British Rail – was redundant almost from the moment it was completed, as rail freight was increasingly transferred to the roads (cutting out the train journey in between). Originally it survived as a place for raves, admired by Nicholas Serota whose team recorded the art found in the building. It's a building that's survived because it could accommodate a multitude of formal and very informal uses (the last rave there lasted four days!), but also because of its memorable form.

This is important. My argument for the universal building is not anti-form; indeed it is quite the opposite. To survive, architecture must make a memorable impression – and neither being dictated to by use nor nailing on an image by way of an elevation is enough.

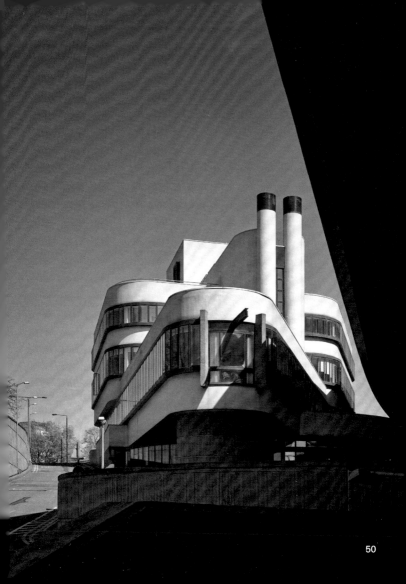

Our headquarters for Cathedral took the space from worship to work. Now we are reworking it to house an apartment and restaurant.

51

Horseferry has become a house of fashion rather than government.

DEAN RYLE
STREET SW1
CITY OF WESTMINSTER

52

Scotland Yard has been home to an ever-changing suite of institutions, and in this incarnation it is once again the home of the Metropolitan Police.

Our two gallery projects – the Saatchi and 176 – had alternative uses before becoming places for art. The Saatchi building was an orphanage from the eighteenth century, before being used by the Territorial Army for military purposes. And when we found it was about to be demised and reconfigured as an office.

176 was originally built as a Methodist church. It later housed a drama school and theatre, and it's now a gallery. A gallery that acknowledges the liberating force of history by leaving successive exhibition curators to work within the found place.

174
Prince of Wales
Road

Regent Street was composed of thin slivers of office stacked over retail sheds, each constituent part built separately behind grand and imposing facades that themselves had, in turn, replaced Nash's more elegant if less imposing facades. All this is also adjacent to older terraced houses that have now been conjoined and adapted for a mixture of uses.

And then there's the Tea Building, which is in fact three separate and different buildings and a dodgy boozer (which, in this never-ending project, is soon to become the entrance to a new building on the roof).
It was built as a bacon factory for Lipton's Teas, and then became a storage warehouse. We have since discovered that spaces within the building, perhaps unsurprisingly, reflect long-forgotten layouts in the original factory 'fit-out'. So, for example, the original workers' canteen is mirrored by advertising agency Mother's 'radical new layout'.

Tea has become a memorable place, a place that people want to go to for reasons that have nothing to do with the architecture of the building. Its success is founded upon the ad hoc, the incidental and the incremental: it's a collage city.

This study into how extra ordinary architecture is made from the ordinary has led us to conclude that our strategy must be to make the generic specific to current use without in any way precluding further uses in an unknowable future.

You make new places and you make them bespoke, not just in spatial terms but because the people that use them will use them in different ways. You make memorable sequences of specific spaces that connect more loosely defined, generic spaces. Of course, these in turn must still have volume, light and character.

Early patrons of the tailors on London's Savile Row, built between 1731 and 1735 as part of the Burlington Estate, would choose or 'bespeak' a particular length of material for their clothes. As the street's reputation grew, the word bespoke came to mean a suit custom tailored, cut and made by hand to the very specific taste – and proportions – of the customer.

SAVILE ROW W.1

If we do this, people will always respond positively to an architecture and work to make these generic spaces specific to their particular needs at their particular moment.

Our architecture is about making the readymade bespoke.

# Image Credits

1  Exterior of Spring Street; Judd Foundation /Licensed by VAGA, New York; Paul Katz

2  Seagram Building, New York City; Architect: Mies van der Rohe with Philip Johnson; Ezra Stoller/Esto

3  Entrance to Crown Hall, Illinois Institute of Technology, Chicago; Architect: Mies van der Rohe; Architectural Press Archive /RIBA Collections

4  (and cover) Casa del Fascio (Palazzo Terragni), Como; Architect: Giuseppe Terragni; Keita Ebidzuka

5  The Bradbury Building interior; Architect: Sumner Hunt, George Wyman; Richard Hartog/ Getty Images

6  Philp Johnson, Ludwig Mies van der Rohe and Phyllis Lambert in front of an image of the model for the Seagram Building, New York, 1955; Phyllis Lambert fonds, Collection Centre Canadien d'Architecture/Canadian Centre for Architecture, Montréal; © United Press International

7  At work on London's skyscraper [the new headquarters for London Underground, which when completed was the tallest building in London], October 1928; Planet News Archive/ Getty Images

8  Central Park Stroll; Hulton Archive/ Getty Images

9  The naked city : illustration de hypothèse des plagues tournantes en psychogéographique, c.1957; G.E. Debord General Collection, Beinecke Rare Book and Manuscript Library, Yale University

10  Traffic Study, project, Philadelphia, Pennsylvania. Plan of proposed traffic-movement pattern, 1952; Louis I. Kahn; Digital image, The Museum of Modern Art, New York/Scala, Florence

11  Artist Agnes Denes in a field of wheat; John McGrail/The LIFE Images Collection/Getty Images

12  Standing Proud [St Paul's Cathedral standing above surrounding burning buildings during the London blitz], 1941; Herbert Mason/Daily Mail/ Getty Images

13  Cabinet maker in Shoreditch, 1940s; Mary Evans Picture Library/Photo Union Collection

14  Extract from The County of London Plan, 1945; EJ Carter and Ernö Goldfinger; Courtesy of Penguin Books

15  A March to the Bank, 1787; James Gillray Courtesy of the Warden and Scholars of New College, Oxford/ Bridgeman Images

16  Universal Use Class Orders, 2012; Allford Hall Monaghan Morris (with thanks to Her Majesty's Stationery Office)

17  Home Time [workers leaving the Camperdown Mills in Dundee], 1955; John Murray/Getty Images

18  Detail of the Tea Building, London; Timothy Soar

19  Built Form Studies from Urban Space and Structures, 1972; Lionel March; Courtesy of Cambridge University Press

20  Drawing from Garden Cities of Tomorrow, 1902; Sir Ebenezer Howard; RIBA Collections

This book is based on a talk given at the Allford Hall Monaghan Morris (AHMM) Spring Conference in 2015 and further developed in a lecture at the Royal Institute of British Architects (RIBA) in December 2015.

It also draws upon the vital conversations that began among the four of us (Jonathan Hall, Paul Monaghan, Peter Morris and I) when we were developing our joint thesis at the Bartlett School of Architecture in 1985. Two key statements of position defined the way ahead for both that project and for the following thirty years of collaboration: firstly, that 'it is in the field of everyday building that modern architecture has failed the city' and secondly, that 'functional programme alone is not sufficient to generate an architecture'.

The challenge to us then, as now, was how to pursue a modern architecture, capable of aggregation, that could create urban public space, without reliance on the prop of historic fabric as context and, importantly and particularly, utilising the everyday buildings that form the underlying matrix of the city.

Thank you to Andy Stevens and Tom Finn at Graphic Thought Facility for making this small book out of our big ideas, and David Dunster at the Bartlett for showing us how boring can become good.

Cover image: Casa del Fascio/Casa del Popolo/ad infinitum
(AHMM, with thanks to Keita Ebidzuka and Graphic Thought Facility)

Extra Ordinary
Copyright © 2016 FifthMan
FifthMan, c/o Allford Hall Monaghan Morris,
Morelands, 5-23 Old Street, London EC1V 9HL, UK

ISBN 978-0-9934378-0-9

First published in 2016 by FifthMan
Reprinted 2019

Editor: Emma Keyte